Animal Kingdom

INSECTS

by Janet Riehecky

Consultant: Jackie Gai, DVM
Wildlife Veterinarian

raintree
a Capstone company — publishers for children

Raintree is an imprint of Capstone Global Library Limited, a company incorporated in England and Wales having its registered office at 264 Banbury Road, Oxford, OX2 7DY – Registered company number: 6695582

www.raintree.co.uk
myorders@raintree.co.uk

Edited by Kathryn Clay
Designed by Rick Korab and Juliette Peters
Picture research by Kelly Garvin
Production by Gene Bentdahl
Originated by Capstone Global Library LTD
Printed and bound in China.

ISBN 978 1 4747 3458 5
21 20 19 18 17
10 9 8 7 6 5 4 3 2 1

British Library Cataloguing in Publication Data
A full catalogue record for this book is available from the British Library.

Acknowledgements
We would like to thank the following for permission to reproduce photographs: Shutterstock: 4Pound, 22 (t), Akil Rolle-Rowan, 19 (b), Aleksei Verhovski, 27 (b), anat chant, 17 (tl), Anatolich, back cover, 28 (t), Andrea Mangoni, 29 (b), Andrey Pavlov (1 (tr), 8-9, AustralianCamera, 13 (br), bluedog studio, 25 (b), Bonnie Taylor Barry, 1 (l), 8 (l), Cathy Keifer, 17 (br), Chaikom, 24 (b), 31 (tl), chakkrachai nicharat, 26-27, charnsitr, 13 (tr), Cheng Wei, 14 (tl), Chik_77, 20-21, corlaffra, 14-15, Cornel Constanin, 26 (t), Craig Taylor, 23 (bl), Daniel Prudek, 31 (bl), Dario Lo Presti, 24 (t), Decha Thapanya, 15 (bl), devil79d, 9 (tl), Dr. Morley Read, 16 (b), Ehrman Photographic, cover, (br), encikAn, 4-5, Eric Isselee, 28 (b), FCG, 13 (bl), Feng Lu, 16-17, fotohunter, 11 (bl), Fotokostic, 27 (tr), Four Oaks, 30 (tl), Geza Farkas, 15 (tr), Gregory A. Pozhvanov, 12 (b), Henrik Larsson, 20 (b), 26 (b), IanRedding, 9 (tr), Irina Kozorog, 29 (t), ittipon, 23-23, ivvv1975, 32, Jack Hong, 19 (t), Johan Larson, 22 (b), john Michael evan potter, 17 (tr), Joseph Calev, 25 (t), kingfisher, 23 (br), Klanarong Chitmung, 27 (tl), Lehrer, 1 (br), 15 (br), LFRabanedo, 12 (t), Lightspring, 30 (br), Malafo, 14 (b), Mamontova Yulia, 10-11, MarcelClemens, 10 (b), Mathisa, 11 (br), Mau Horng, 10 (t), mchin, 16 (t), Menno Schaefer, 24-25, MMCez, cover (bl), noppasit TH, 4 (inset), Olga Bogatyrenko, 16 (m), Orapin Joyphuem, 23 (t), pan demin, cover (tl), 21 (r), Patrick Foto, 9 (b), Production Perig, cover, (tr), Rainer Fuhrmann, 5 (inset), RugliG, 17 (b), Simun Ascic, 12-13, skynetphoto, 30 (bl), Smit, 15 (tl), Starover Sibiriak, 31 (tr), sujesh, 31 (br), SW_Stock, 30 (tr), tcareob72, 11 (t), Thithawat.S, 28-29, Tobias Zehndbauer, 6-7, TOMPOST, 21 (l), Tomatito, 18-19, 18 (l), Vadim Petrakov, 13 (tl), Vladimir Wrangel, 14 (tr)

Artistic elements: Shutterstock: AlexGreenArt, Kuttelvaserova Stuchelova

Every effort has been made to contact copyright holders of material reproduced in this book. Any omissions will be rectified in subsequent printings if notice is given to the publisher.

CONTENTS

What are insects?

Insects are animals with sectioned bodies and six legs. They usually have one or two pairs of wings too. Insects are the largest group of animals on Earth. About 90 per cent of all animals are insects.

class
a smaller group of living things; insects are in the class Insecta

kingdom
one of five very large groups into which all living things are placed; the two main kingdoms are plants and animals; insects belong to the animal kingdom

phylum
(FIE-lum)
a group of living things with a similar body plan; insects belong to the phylum Arthropoda (ar-THROP-uh-duh); arachnids and crustaceans are also in this group

arthropod
(AR-thruh-pod)
an invertebrate with many body sections; insects, crustaceans and arachnids are arthropods

cold-blooded
also called ectothermic (EK-tuh-THER-mik) cold-blooded animals have a body temperature that is the same as the air around them; insects are cold-blooded

invertebrate
(in-VUR-tuh-brut)
an animal without a backbone; more than 97 per cent of animals are invertebrates, including insects

species
(SPEE-sees)
a group of animals that are alike and can produce young with each other; there are more than 1 million species of insects

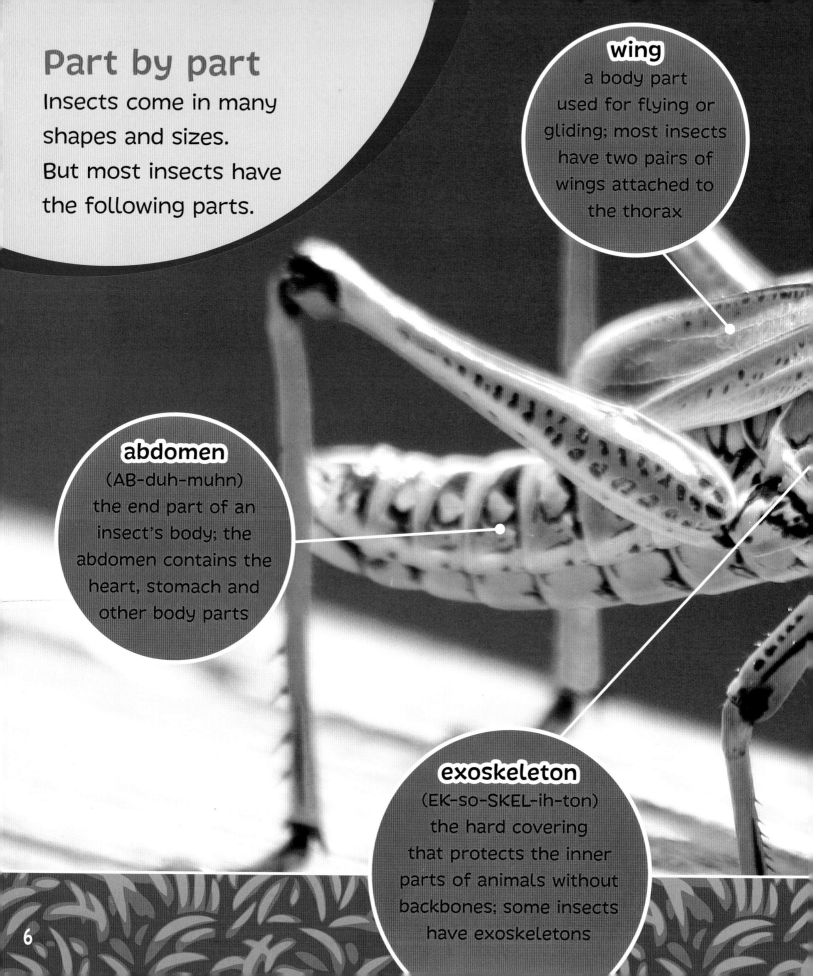

Part by part

Insects come in many shapes and sizes. But most insects have the following parts.

wing
a body part used for flying or gliding; most insects have two pairs of wings attached to the thorax

abdomen
(AB-duh-muhn) the end part of an insect's body; the abdomen contains the heart, stomach and other body parts

exoskeleton
(EK-so-SKEL-ih-ton) the hard covering that protects the inner parts of animals without backbones; some insects have exoskeletons

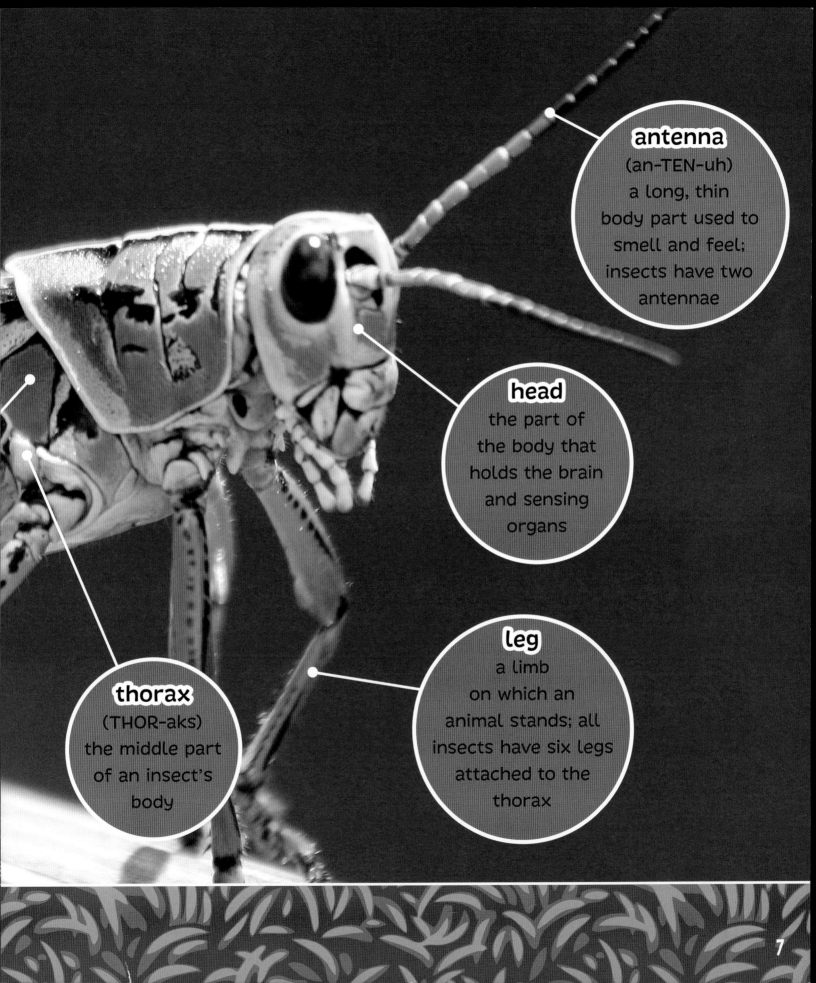

antenna
(an-TEN-uh)
a long, thin
body part used to
smell and feel;
insects have two
antennae

head
the part of
the body that
holds the brain
and sensing
organs

thorax
(THOR-aks)
the middle part
of an insect's
body

leg
a limb
on which an
animal stands; all
insects have six legs
attached to the
thorax

Common groups

cicada
(sih-KAY-duh)
an insect with large eyes, a thick body and four wings; cicadas live under ground and come out once every 13 to 17 years

bee
has a thick, hairy body with four wings and a stinger; bees feed on a sweet liquid called nectar and live in large groups

wasp
similar to a bee but with less hair and a slimmer shape

dragonfly
a long, thin insect with two pairs of wings

ant
lives in tunnels under ground; ants are related to wasps and bees

fly
has two wings and hairy, sticky feet; gnats and mosquitoes are also flies

louse

a small, oval-shaped insect without wings; lice feed on blood

beetle

beetles make up more than 40 per cent of all insects; ladybirds, fireflies and lightning bugs are beetles

butterfly

has a thin body with large, colourful wings; butterflies are active during the day

moth

similar to a butterfly but with a thicker body and less colourful wings; moths are active at night

cricket

a black or brown insect with strong hind legs; male crickets rub their front wings together to make sound

Circle of life

All insects start out as eggs. Some female insects lay their eggs in nests. Others carry them in their bodies and give birth to live young.

pupa
(PYOO-puh): the life stage between a larva and an adult when the insect is covered in a casing

egg
the first stage of life for most insects

life cycle
the series of changes that take place in a living thing, from birth to death

mate
to join together to make young

larva
(LAR-vuh): the second stage of life for some insects; caterpillars are a kind of larva

live young
babies born directly from their mother, rather than from laid eggs; some cockroaches give birth to live young

cocoon

(kuh-KOON): a soft covering that protects an insect during the pupa stage

nymph

(NIMF): a young insect that is not yet an adult

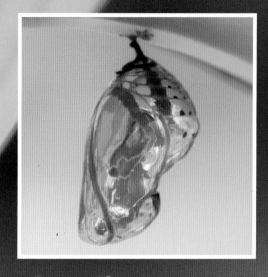

chrysalis

(KRIS-uh-lis): a butterfly in its pupa stage; the hard chrysalis casing often hangs from a leaf or twig

moult

to shed; many larvae must shed their hard skin; some insects moult up to 60 times during their lifetime

metamorphosis

(met-uh-MOR-fuh-sis): the process of changing from a young animal to an adult animal

A place to call home

Insects live on every land mass and in every body of water on Earth.

habitat

the type of place and conditions in which a plant or animal lives; insects live in many different habitats, including deserts, rainforests and oceans

desert

(DEH-zuhrt): a dry area that gets little rain; blue-winged grasshoppers live in rocky desert hills

tundra

(TUN-druh): a large, flat area of land found in the Arctic; no trees grow in the tundra, and the ground is always frozen: Arctic bumblebees and mosquitoes live in the tundra

mound

termites mix saliva with soil to make mud mounds; the mounds sit above underground tunnels

hive

a nest for bees; bees make hives in trees or holes in rocks

nest

a structure built by animals to hold their eggs; wasps make paper nests from chewed wood and spit

rainforest

a thick area of trees where rain falls almost every day; scientists believe most of the world's insects live in rainforests

Working together

plague
(PLAYG)
a group of
locusts

flock
a group
of lice

worker
an insect that
gathers food and
builds the colony;
workers cannot
mate

cloud
a group of
grasshoppers

swarm
a large
group; insects
fly together to
form swarms

soldier
an insect that keeps the colony safe; soldiers are larger and heavier than workers

intrusion
a group of cockroaches

army
a group of caterpillars

queen
the only female in a colony that lays eggs

colony
(KOLL-luh-nee)
a big group of insects that live and work together; millions of termites can live in a single colony

Let's eat

Insects eat almost anything. Some eat plants. Others eat meat or blood. Some even eat rotting wood or fungus!

herbivore

(HUR-buh-vor): an animal that eats only plants; many insects are herbivores

predator

(PRED-uh-tur): an animal that hunts other animals for food; tiger beetles are predators

prey

(PRAY): an animal hunted by another animal for food; insects are the prey of many animals, including spiders, frogs, birds and fish

carnivore

(KAHR-nuh-vor): an animal that eats only meat; the praying mantis eats other insects

proboscis

(pruh-BOSS-sis): a long sucking tube in the mouth; butterflies and moths use a proboscis to eat

nectar
(NEK-ter): a sweet liquid found in flowers; bees drink nectar

dung
an animal's waste; dung beetles eat the dung of other animals

scavenger
(SKAV-in-jer): an animal that feeds on animals that are already dead; desert ants are scavengers

milkweed
a type of plant with a milky sap; milkweed is a monarch caterpillar's only food source

Sensing the world

Insects use their senses to understand the world around them. But their senses don't always work like humans'. Butterflies, for example, taste with their feet!

ears
grasshoppers and crickets have ears on their legs

compound eye
many tiny eyes that work together; compound eyes allow insects to see in almost every direction

ultraviolet
a colour some insects see, but people can't; bees see ultraviolet patterns on flowers that lead them to the flowers' nectar

taste receptor

(TAYST ri-SEP-tur): a tiny sensor that senses flavours; insects can taste salty, bitter, sweet and sour flavours

electric charge

a signal a bee makes on a flower by flapping its wings; the electric charge stays on the flower so other bees don't visit it again

sensory hairs

stiff hairs that help insects sense things such as air movement; male mosquitoes have sensory hairs on their antennae that help them hear female mosquitoes

smell

helps insects find food or a mate; a male silkmoth can smell a female 9.7 kilometres (6 miles) away

Move it!

Insects move in all sorts of ways. Some use their six legs to run or crawl. Others use wings to fly.

jump
grasshoppers can jump a distance 20 times longer than their own body

wiggle
to move by twisting from side to side; when silverfish wiggle, they look like swimming fish

fly
flies usually travel about 7 km (4.5 miles) per hour; they can have a burst of speed up to 24 km (15 miles) per hour if in danger

march
to walk with a steady pace; army ants usually march in a straight line

sway
to move back and forth; praying mantises copy the movement of swaying leaves; doing so makes the insects harder to see

swim
whirligig beetles swim in circles on the water's surface

Staying safe

Insects do many things to escape danger. Some insects move faster than predators. Others trick predators or fight back.

run away
the most common way for insects to stay safe; cockroaches can run 1.5 metres (5 feet) per second

curl up
cuckoo wasps curl into balls to keep their heads safe

camouflage
(KA-muh-flahzh) colouring that makes animals look like their surroundings; walking sticks look like twigs; camouflage helps them hide in plain sight

play dead
some insects, such as giant water bugs, play dead; some predators won't eat animals they think are dead

stink
some insects release a stinky smell when in danger

mimicry
(MIM-ih-kree)
the act of looking like something or someone else; if a hawk moth caterpillar sees a predator, it pulls in its legs and head and swells to look like a snake

shoot spray
a bombardier beetle can shoot a boiling hot spray at a predator

stinger
a sharp, pointed organ; bees and wasps use their stingers to stick predators

Helpful insects

From honey to silk, insects make many useful products. Insects are also important for helping plants to grow.

silk

the soft fibre made by caterpillars called silkworms; some clothes are made of silk

cochineal

(KOH-chuh-neel): a tiny, fuzzy insect; female cochineals make a red dye that's used to add colouring to food, make-up and paint

decompose

(dee-kuhm-POHZ): to break down plant or animal material; some insects help wood and dead matter decompose by eating it

consumer
(kuhn-SOO-mer): an animal that needs to eat other things for energy; ladybirds can eat up to 60 aphids each day

pollen
a yellow powder that helps plants make seeds and fruit; bees move pollen from one flower to another so fruits and vegetables can grow

beeswax
made by bees for honey storage cells; people use beeswax to keep food from spoiling; beeswax is also used in some beauty products, candles and crayons

honey
a sweet substance used as a spread or in cooking; honey is made from the nectar collected by bees

Not-so-helpful insects

Most insects are harmless to humans. A few, though, can be harmful to people and plants.

malaria
a disease that can cause fever, vomiting and sometimes death; malaria is spread through mosquito bites

aphids
(AY-fids)
small insects that eat garden plants

infest
to take over in large numbers; termites and wood-boring beetles can infest and eat the wood in people's houses

beetle

venom
(VEN-uhm)
a poison that some animals make; fire ants bite and sting to release their venom; the venom causes a burning feeling on the skin

crops
plants grown for food or other human use; many insects eat crops, hurting people's jobs

allergy
(AL-er-jee)
something that causes a person to cough, sneeze or have trouble breathing; some people are allergic to bee stings or fire ant bites

rash
red spots on the skin caused by a reaction to something; the hairs from a browntail moth caterpillar can cause painful rashes

Insect records

loudest insect
the calling sound of the African cicada is so loud it can hurt people's ears

fastest flyer
horseflies can fly 145 kilometres (90 miles) per hour

shortest life
one type of mayfly lives only a few minutes as an adult; it is alive just long enough to mate and lay eggs

longest insect
stick insects can grow to be 36 centimetres (14.2 inches) long

heaviest insect
the giant weta can weigh 71 grams (2.5 ounces)

deadliest venom
a type of harvester ant can kill a rat

biggest wingspan
the atlas moth measures 30 cm (12 inches) from wingtip to wingtip

fastest runner
Australian tiger beetles can move 2.5 metres (5.6 miles) per hour

fastest wings
sandflies beat their wings about 1,045 times a second

longest life as an adult
some African mound-building termite queens live more than 60 years

biggest insect
titan beetles (*Titanus giganteus*) can measure up to 16.8 cm (6.6 inches) long and 7.6 cm (3 inches) wide

strongest insect
the horned dung beetle can pull an object 1,141 times its own body weight

Fun facts

The **horned dung beetle** rolls dung into a ball and buries it to eat later. It can bury 250 times its own weight in one night.

Mosquitoes have lived on Earth for 400 million years. Only female mosquitoes bite people.

Cockroaches can live for more than one week without their head. They also have white blood. Most insects have yellow blood.

The **praying mantis** is the only insect that can turn its head from side to side.

A **queen termite** can lay 40,000 eggs in a single day.

The lens is the part of the eye that focuses light and makes clear images. **Dragonflies** can have 30,000 lenses in each eye.

A **bee** needs to make about 10 million flights to get enough nectar to make just 454 grams (1 pound) of honey.

A **locust** eats its own body weight in plants every day.

FIND OUT MORE

Bugs (Record Busters), Clive Gifford (Wayland, 2016)

Insects and Spiders (Visual Explorers), Paul Calver and Toby Reynolds (Franklin Watts, 2016)

Smithsonian Super Bug Encyclopedia, John Woodward (DK, 2016)

WEBSITES

animals.nationalgeographic.com/animals/bugs
Pictures, videos and facts about all kinds of insects.

www.bbc.co.uk/nature/life/Insect/by/rank/all
Visit this website to find videos and information about 80 different insects.

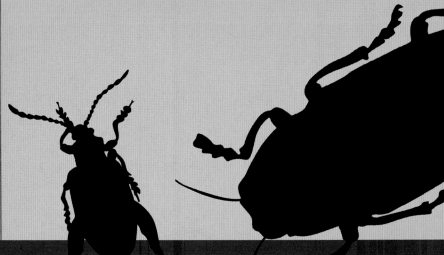